Fathoming
Bethlehem

I searched
God's lexicon
To fathom "Bethlehem"
And "Calvary." It simply said:
See "Love."

—GORDON GILSDORF

Fathoming

Bethlehem

ADVENT MEDITATIONS

Robert F. Morneau

A Crossroad Book
The Crossroad Publishing Company
New York

1997

The Crossroad Publishing Company
370 Lexington Avenue, New York, NY 10017

Copyright © 1997 by Robert F. Morneau

Printed in the United States of America

Acknowledgments will be found on pages 107–08, which
constitute an extension of the copyright page.

Library of Congress Cataloging-in-Publication Data

Morneau, Robert F., 1938–
    Fathoming Bethlehem : Advent meditations / Robert F.
Morneau
        p.   cm.
    ISBN 0-8245-1689-3
    1. Advent—Meditations. 2. Catholic Church—Prayer-
books and devotions—English. 3. Devotional calendars—
Catholic Church. I. Title.
    BX2170.A4M67 1997
    242'.332—dc21   97-15538
                                                                CIP

CONTENTS

PREFACE

Advent has a rich vocabulary: expectancy, longing, preparation, coming. More deeply, Advent has a great treasure: the Lord Jesus! All who profess the Christian faith have a relationship to this joyful liturgical season. A central question each of us should attempt to answer: "Where will you advent this year?"

The poet Jessica Powers gives her answer:

ADVENT

I live my Advent in the womb of Mary.
And on one night when a great star swings free
from its high mooring and walks down the sky
to be the dot above the *Christus I,*
I shall be born of her by blessed grace.
I wait in Mary-darkness, faith's walled place,
with hope's expectance of nativity.

I knew for long she carried me and fed me,
guarded and loved me, though I could not see.
But only now, with inward jubilee,
I come upon earth's most amazing knowledge:
someone is hidden in this dark with me.

Jessica Powers

As we journey in community toward the Christmas mystery, we do so as a prayerful people. Prayer is paying attention. Prayer is an act of intentionality by which we attune ourselves to that Someone hidden within our souls and who transcends all time and space. We ponder the word of God and seek to

7

respond to it in praise and thanksgiving. We join our personal prayer to the voice of the worshiping community in an acknowl- edgment of our loving and providential God. Advent is a sea- son of serious conversation and tender intimacy.

Besides scripture and our vast traditions of specific prayers, our Advent time of preparation and expectancy might also be enriched by the poets. This singing band of pilgrims is unique in their love for language and in their gifts of insight and articulation. As Evelyn Underhill reminds us:

> Moreover, poetry both enchants and informs, address- ing its rhythmic and symbolic speech to regions of the mind which are inaccessible to argument, and evoking movements of awe and love which no exhortation can obtain. It has meaning at many levels, and welds together all those who use it; overriding their personal moods and subduing them to its grave loveliness.

We need once again to be enchanted and informed. Our culture makes us cynics; poetry restores hope. The explosion of knowledge and our frenetic activism cause us to forget the essentials of our lives. Poetry re-teaches us the fundamentals of life. Advent is a season to be fascinated once again by God's gracious love.

Poetry has a power that argumentation and exhortation lack. Poems evoke wonder and awe. Through images and inner rhythm, the mind is transformed at hidden and deep levels. Advent is a season of love, not logic. Religious poets keep pointing us toward the star above Bethlehem.

During this liturgical season we journey together. What binds us to the community in a special way are our songs and poems. They weld us together in that they carry our sense of identity and contain the truths we believe. Certain phrases and stanzas sinks deeply into our souls, get stuck there, and cannot get out. Their grave loveliness is cause for joy and beauty.

The reader of this slim volume is asked to do a number of things:

1. Read the scripture passage indicated for each day of Advent. Ponder the word of God slowly and prayerfully. Meditate on it for five minutes or so.

2. Look over the contextual paragraph and the refrain (the antiphon from Vespers service of the Divine Office).

3. Read out loud the poem; read it twice with different emphases.

4. Study the commentary and select a question to carry with you throughout the day. In the evening write out your answer in the margins.

5. Conclude your prayer time by praying with the Church.

One of the basic principles of life is to begin every activity or project with the goal in mind. The Latin adage reads: *"In omnibus respice finem!"* ("In all things, look to the end!") Great wisdom here. Advent's end is Nativity. Advent has meaning only insofar as it gets us to the mystery of Bethlehem. And when we arrive, will we find birth or death, or both? As Jessica Powers's "Advent" speaks of our interior journey, T. S. Eliot's "Journey of the Magi" tells of the outer terrain. Both enchant and inform, evoke and remind us of mystery: the mystery of God-made-man. The mystery of Emmanuel.

JOURNEY OF THE MAGI

"A cold coming we had of it,
Just the worst time of the year
For a journey, and such a long journey:
The ways deep and the weather sharp,
The very dead of winter."
And the camels galled, sore-footed, refractory,
Lying down in the melting snow.
There were times we regretted
The summer palaces on slopes, the terraces,
And the silken girls bringing sherbet.
Then the camel men cursing and grumbling
And running away, and wanting their liquor and women,
And the night-fires going out, and lack of shelters,
And cities hostile and the towns unfriendly
And the villages dirty and charging high prices:
A hard time we had of it.
At the end we preferred to travel all night,
Sleeping in snatches,
With the voices singing in our ears, saying
That this was all folly.

Then at dawn we came down to a temperate valley,
Wet, below the snow line, smelling of vegetation,
With a running stream and a water-mill beating the darkness
And three trees on the low sky.
And an old white horse galloped away in the meadow.
Then we came to a tavern with vine-leaves over the lintel,
Six hands at an open door dicing for pieces of silver,
And feet kicking the empty wine-skins.
But there was no information, and so we continued

And arrived at evening, not a moment too soon
Finding the place; it was (you may say) satisfactory.

All this was a long time ago, I remember,
And I would do it again, but set down
This set down
This: were we led all that way for
Birth or Death? There was a Birth, certainly,
We had evidence and no doubt. I had seen birth and death,
But had thought they were different; this Birth was
Hard and bitter agony for us, like Death, our death.
We returned to our places, these Kingdoms,
But no longer at ease here, in the old dispensation,
With an alien people clutching their gods.
I should be glad of another death.

T. S. Eliot

FIRST WEEK OF ADVENT

FIRST SUNDAY of ADVENT
Matthew 24:37–44 (A); Matthew 13:33–37 (B)
Luke 21:25–28 (C)

The Gospel imperatives are clear: Be on guard! Stay awake! Be alert to the unexpected coming of our God. Advent is a season of attentiveness. It is also a season of accountability. We have been given a trust and a set of responsibilities that makes us stewards and servants of the mysteries of God. We don't have to wait four weeks to encounter our God. The Lord breaks into our lives today in word and historical events, in the needs of our sisters and brothers. If we stay awake, if we are on guard, we will be able to give a favorable account of the stewardship entrusted to us.

Refrain: "Do not be afraid, Mary, you have found favor with God; you will conceive and give birth to a Son, alleluia."

> The wind, one brilliant day, called
> to my soul with an aroma of jasmine.
>
> "In return for this jasmine odor,
> I'd like all the odor of your roses."

12

"I have no roses; I have no flowers left now
in my garden. . . . All are dead."

"Then I'll take the waters of the fountains,
and the yellow leaves and the dried up petals."

The wind left. . . . I wept. I said to my soul,
"What have you done with the garden entrusted to you?"

Antonio Machado

When the Holy Spirit called to the soul of Mary, asking her what she had done to the garden entrusted to her, we know the answer. Mary was on guard and alert. Mary was obedient and self-giving. Her garden, the child Jesus, received from her extravagant love and faithful protection.

We, on the other hand, have not fared as well. We have failed to be on guard against temptation and sin. We have refused God's wishes and have lived seasons of our lives in rebellion. The wind has found our garden empty and barren at times. We need again to recommit ourselves to the seeds of grace that daily are given to us.

As we enter this graced season we have an intercessor in heaven. We need but turn to Mary with sincerity of heart, tasting each word of the "Ave Maria": ". . . pray for us sinners, now, and at the hour of our death." Through Mary's assistance, we may one day not weep over our garden, but rejoice in its beautiful harvest of peace, justice, and joy.

1. How alert am I to the wind of the Holy Spirit who daily stirs in my life?

2. What is the present condition of my garden?

3. In return for the aroma of God's grace, what have I given to the Lord?

Praying with the Church
    Father in heaven,
    our hearts desire the warmth of your love
    and our minds are searching for the light of your Word.
    Increase our longing for Christ our Savior
    and give us the strength to grow in love,
    that the dawn of his coming
    may find us rejoicing in his presence
    and welcoming the light of his truth.
    We ask this in the name of Jesus the Lord.

MONDAY of the FIRST WEEK of ADVENT
Matthew 8:5–11

Jesus was amazed at the deep faith and tender compassion of the centurion who was so concerned about his sick servant boy. And note Jesus' prompt response to the request. "I will come and cure him." As we enter this first week of Advent we too have requests and Jesus hears our every word. We need but ask in faith and we are assured of God's saving presence.

Refrain: "The angel of the Lord brought God's message to Mary, and she conceived by the power of the Holy Spirit, alleluia."

Last night, as I was sleeping,
I dreamt—marvellous error!—
that a spring was breaking
out in my heart.
I said: Along which secret aqueduct,
Oh water, are you coming to me,
water of a new life
that I have never drunk?

Last night, as I was sleeping,
I dreamt—marvellous error!—
that I had a beehive
here inside my heart.
And the golden bees
were making white combs
and sweet honey
from my old failures.

Last night, as I was sleeping,
I dreamt—marvellous error!—
that a fiery sun was giving
light inside my heart.
It was fiery because I felt
warmth as from a hearth,
and sun because it gave light
and brought tears to my eyes.

Last night, as I slept,
I dreamt—marvellous error!—
that it was God I had
here inside my heart.

Antonio Machado

After meeting Jesus, I wonder if the centurion began having strange dreams. Did he dream about a new life springing from a well of compassion and love? The curing of the sick boy was surely new life. No wonder the centurion felt so unworthy in the presence of so much goodness.

Did the centurion, having encountered Jesus, dream further about the mystery of redemption? Is it possible that our old failures can be transformed from ugliness into things of beauty? Perhaps there is a beehive in all of our hearts if only we had the faith to believe.

Perhaps, in the curing of the servant boy, the centurion cried out with joy and felt warmth within his heart. Maybe new dreams of a fiery sun filled his nights and made them holy. No illusions here but *marvellous* truth.

1. Why has God made his home within my heart?

2. What attributes of the Trinity are found in the images of spring, beehive, and fiery sun?

3. Who is the God of my daydreams?

Praying with the Church
   Lord our God,
   help us to prepare
   for the coming of Christ your Son.
   May he find us waiting,
   eager in joyful prayer.
   We ask this through our Lord Jesus Christ, your Son,
   who lives and reigns with you and the Holy Spirit,
   one God, for ever and ever.

TUESDAY of the FIRST WEEK of ADVENT
Luke 10:21–24

A dvent is a season of special revelation. But unless we see and hear through the power of the Holy Spirit, the mysteries of God will remain hidden. Learning and cleverness are no guarantee for knowing the things of God. Rather, the simplicity of small children is the disposition that opens us to whole new worlds.

Refrain: "Seek the Lord while he may be found; call on him while he is near, alleluia."

In the shady parts of the square, moss
is growing, and on the sacred old slabs
of the church. A beggar stands on the church porch. . . .
He has a soul older than the church.

On the cold mornings he climbs with tremendous slowness
up the marble stairs
toward a stony nook—then the dry hand
appears from his torn cloak.

He has seen, with the dusty sockets
of his eyes,
the white shadows go by, in the sun-filled days,
the white shadows of the holy hours.
Antonio Machado

Beggars and children have something in common: an emptiness. This poverty contains a happy grace, a vulnerability to revelation. The beggar sees through the dusty sockets of his eyes the revelation of white shadows, the shadows of holy hours. Indeed, blessed are the poor in spirit.

The beggar stands on the church porch, near God. And God meets the beggar in the stony nook, on a cold morning. Two old souls commingling as time turns into eternity.

We are all beggars. Life is all grace. We need to climb slowly the stairs leading to God. We must not hide behind our learning or cleverness, our security and social roles, our illusions of autonomy. In our poverty we will be filled with the sunshine of grace.

1. In what kinds of situations do I depend on wit or cleverness?

2. Why is it that I often do not see the glory of God that fills the earth?

3. Does the image of beggar sit well with me? Why or why not?

Praying with the Church
> God of mercy and consolation,
> help us in our weakness and free us from sin.
> Hear our prayers
> that we may rejoice at the coming of your Son,
> who lives and reigns with you and the Holy Spirit,
> one God, for ever and ever.

WEDNESDAY of the FIRST WEEK of ADVENT
Matthew 15:29–37

Hardness of heart is a deadly disease. When this malady besets the soul, we fail to tend to the suffering, we neglect to feed the hungry. Jesus' heart is moved with pity as he encounters the sick, the lame, the famished. His compassion overflows into action as he does his ministry of curing and feeding.

Refrain: "The law will go forth from Zion; the word of the Lord from Jerusalem."

> I love Jesus, who said to us:
> Heaven and earth will pass away.
> When heaven and earth have passed away,
> my word will remain.
> What was your word, Jesus?
> Love? Affection? Forgiveness?
> All your words were
> one word: Wakeup.

Antonio Machado

One of Jesus' words is "love"! That word continually becomes incarnate as the Lord reaches out into the lives of those in need. This word connotes active concern, tender respect, a deep self-giving. It is a word easy to say but one that demands enormous energy. Translating love into life was his ministry.

A second word in Jesus' lived vocabulary: "affection." Jesus loved people. His heart stirs at the sight of the suffering and his anger flares when the Father's will is violated.

Affection creates energy and passion. An Advent heart is one that stands on tiptoe, eager to assist whoever is in need.

Forgiveness is more than a word for Jesus; it is a way of life. In curing the sick and feeding the hungry, Jesus was involved in a ministry of reconciliation. Through compassionate communion, conversion would soon follow.

In an odd sort of way, love, affection, and forgiveness arise out of a single headwater: attentiveness. Jesus' ministry is essentially a wakeup call.

1. List ten words found in the lexicon of those who follow Jesus.

2. In what way are the lyrics "Don't talk of love, show me!" appropriate for our Advent hymnal?

3. What does an act of kindness do to my heart?

Praying with the Church
Lord our God,
grant that we may be ready
to receive Christ when he comes in glory
and to share in the banquet of heaven,
where he lives and reigns with you and the Holy Spirit,
one God, for ever and ever.

THURSDAY of the FIRST WEEK of ADVENT
Matthew 7:21,24–27

A great Christmas gift to give or receive: wisdom! This grace has a double meaning. First, the wise person knows what is pleasing to God. Here is the door to the kingdom. Second, the wise person does God's will and refuses to remain in the antechamber of just knowing. Advent is a season of wise women and men following the example of Jesus and thereby constructing a spiritual life on solid principles.

Refrain: "Blessed are you among women, and blessed is the fruit of your womb."

> Form your letters slowly and well:
> making things well
> is more important than making them.
> *Antonio Machado*

A good piece of advice. The quality we put into the project of existence is of great significance. Just saying or doing is not sufficient for a truly human life. We must take our time and give each task and each person the appropriate reverence.

Saying "Lord, Lord," is no guarantee that we have embraced the lordship of Jesus or that we are committed to building the kingdom of God. Rather, living the Gospel imperatives in spirit and truth assures us that we are indeed an Advent people.

There is a tendency to get sloppy, to cut corners, to simply get the job done without due regard for its excellence. This is foolishness and borders on stupidity. Constant vigilance is in order and perhaps an outside accountant (read spiritual director) who will keep us focused and serious about living our discipleship deeply and well.

1. Who are several wise individuals who have modeled authentic discipleship for me?

2. Is my spiritual edifice built on rock or sand?

3. Why is the ancient Latin adage *"festine lente"* ("make haste slowly") good Advent advice?

Praying with the Church
Father,
we need your help.
Free us from sin and bring us to life.
Support us by your power.
Grant this through our Lord Jesus Christ, your Son,
who lives and reigns with you and the Holy Spirit,
one God, for ever and ever.

FRIDAY of the FIRST WEEK of ADVENT
Matthew 9:27–31

Most of us visit an optometrist with implicit confidence and faith. This professional is schooled in helping people to see. We leave the office with new contacts or glasses and find the world more focused, sometimes larger than we had previously known. Jesus, our divine optometrist, wants people to see and know, drawing them out of darkness and ignorance into the world of light and grace. All we need to do is request the gift of sight with confidence and faith. Divine compassion will bring us healing.

Refrain: "Out of Egypt I have called my Son; he will come to save his people."

> Is my soul asleep?
> Have those beehives that labor
> at night stopped? And the water
> wheel of thought,
> is it dry, the cups empty,
> wheeling, carrying only shadows?
>
> No my soul is not asleep.
> It is awake, wide awake.
> It neither sleeps nor dreams, but watches,
> its clear eyes open,
> far-off things, and listens
> at the shore of the great silence.
>
> *Antonio Machado*

When we are awake and when our eyes are open, we see far-off things and even things that are near. Jesus came to bring us fullness of life. If our souls are asleep, we fail to notice the advent of grace.

Being wide awake is a constant challenge. So quickly our eyes close and our ears block out sounds seeking our attention. We slip back into darkness, and life continues to pass us by. Even the morning alarm clock struggles to bring us to full attentiveness. Sleepwalking may be more common than imagined.

Someone once said that spirituality is easy to define: "Just stay awake!" But we don't do that of our own accord. The Spirit breaks into our sleep and dreams, continues the beehive labor of turning our failures into sweet honey, bringing the water of new life to our parched souls. The Spirit empowers us to listen "at the shores of the great silence" and there to be embraced by Love.

1. When do I have trouble staying awake? Why?

2. In what way are watchfulness and thoughtfulness first cousins?

3. Do I ever prefer dreams to reality?

Praying with the Church
  Jesus, our Lord,
  save us from our sins.
  Come, protect us from all dangers
  and lead us to salvation,
  for you live and reign with the Father and the Holy Spirit,
  one God, for ever and ever.

SATURDAY of the FIRST WEEK of ADVENT
Matthew 9:35–10:1,6-8

God comes to us under many images: potter *(Jeremiah 18)*, gardener *(Genesis 1)*, friend *(John 15)*. God also comes as a shepherd who is deeply concerned about all sheep, especially those troubled by demons, sickness, fatigue, lostness. One message is to be proclaimed to all of these: "The reign of God is at hand." Advent drives this message home. In Jesus we know the compassion and love of God. Our task is to share the gift given to us—today! That is, we are to share the gift of health, compassion, freedom, and love. A great harvest for all.

Refrain: "Come to us, Lord, and may your presence be our peace; with hearts made perfect we shall rejoice in your companionship for ever."

RAINBOW AT NIGHT
for Don Ramon del Valle-Inclan

The train moves through the Guardarrama
one night on the way to Madrid.
The moon and the fog create
high up a rainbow.
Oh April moon, so calm,
driving the white clouds!

The mother holds her boy
sleeping on her lap.
The boy sleeps, and nevertheless
sees the green fields outside,

and trees lit up by sun,
and the golden butterflies.

The mother, her forehead dark
between a day gone and a day to come,
sees a fire nearly out
and an oven with spiders.

There's a traveler mad with grief,
no doubt seeing odd things;
he talks to himself, and when he looks
wipes us out with his look.

I remember fields under snow,
and pine trees of other mountains.

And you, Lord, through whom we all
have eyes, and who sees souls,
tell us if we all one
day will see your face.

Antonio Machado

The journey is long. As we travel physically and spiritually, we grow weary and face many trials. Jesus had pity on the suffering of people. The exhaustion and fatigue he knew from personal experience.

Despite the night and uncertainty, God's kingdom is near. Rainbows and golden butterflies and green fields whisper of hope and new life. God wants us to care for one another lest the fire, flickering in the heart, goes out.

In the end there is but one question. Will we see the face of God? Will we experience the kingdom? All will be well if we learn a singular lesson: to give to others the gift we have received. And that gift is love. That gift is God.

1. Where have I glimpsed the face of God?

2. What gift have I given away this week?

3. What are some of the clues indicating the nearness of God's reign?

Praying with the Church

God our Father,
you loved the world so much
you gave your only Son to free us
from the ancient power of sin and death.
Help us to wait for his coming,
and lead us to true liberty.
We ask this through our Lord Jesus Christ,
who lives and reigns with you and the Holy Spirit,
one God, for ever and ever.

SECOND WEEK OF ADVENT

SECOND SUNDAY of ADVENT
Matthew 3:1–12 (A); Mark 1:1–8 (B); Luke 3:1–6 (C)

John the Baptist was a person of faith. When God's word came to him, he listened and responded. Into the desert he went to confront his own sinfulness and to call the people of his day to repentance. The wilderness became the geography of grace and from this place he pointed to the coming of someone far greater than he. His whole life was a commitment to preparation, seeking by fasting and simplicity of life to provide lodging for the divine guest. His faith was deep, deeper than death. John the Baptist knew that "this world is not conclusion."

Refrain: "Blessed are you, O Virgin Mary, for your great faith; all that the Lord promised you will come to pass through you."

(501)

This World is not Conclusion.
A Species stands beyond—
Invisible as Music—
But positive, as Sound—
It beckons, and it baffles—

28

Philosophy—don't know—
And through a Riddle, at the last—
Sagacity, must go—
To guess it, puzzles scholars—
To gain it, Men have borne
Contempt of Generations
And Crucifixion, shown—
Faith slips—and laughs, and rallies—
Blushes, if any see—
Plucks at a twig of Evidence—
And asks a Vane, the way—
Much Gesture, from the Pulpit—
Strong Hallelujahs, roll—
Narcotics cannot still the Tooth
That nibbles at the soul—
                                          Emily Dickinson

Advent is a season of faith, a gift that resembles music in its invisibility. Yet for that, it is no less real. Far beyond the wisdom of philosophers and all academicians, faith lies in the land of a radical conviction of God's redeeming love. Some, like John the Baptist or Oscar Romero or the six women killed in central America, have died because of their faith.

Faith is not always steady on her feet. Given our desire for certitude, we do seek assurances and evidence. Doubt is not necessarily a stranger to our souls. Blessed is the person who can still laugh and blush on this long and arduous journey back to God.

Our theologians and preachers are often loud and bold. And rightly so. They do their writing and speaking out of conviction. However, verbal narcotics cannot remove gnawing doubt nor still the trembling before oceanic mystery. Narcotics are useless here. Only a renewal of faith, the kind the Baptist drew upon as he came to the executioner's block, can bring us home.

1. Who was the first person to witness faith to me?

2. Is my faith strong enough to laugh and blush?

3. What "species" stand beyond this world?

Praying with the Church
Father in heaven,
the day draws near when the glory of your Son
will make radiant the night of the waiting world.
May the lure of greed not impede us from the joy
which moves the hearts of those who seek him.
May the darkness not blind us
to the vision of wisdom
which fills the minds of those who find him.
We ask this through Christ our Lord.

MONDAY of the SECOND WEEK of ADVENT
Matthew 9:1–8

Hope is a virtue on the endangered species list. When one has lived years without the fulfillment of desire, discouragement and despair crowd in upon the soul. The paralytic, confined to his bed, must have known times, if not years, of hopelessness. But the man had friends, friends who had faith.

Coming to Jesus, the Lord who came to them, they were astonished at a double healing of body and soul. The paralytic could now walk; more, his sins were forgiven. Good cause here to praise God.

Refrain: "See, your King comes, the master of the earth; he will shatter the yoke of our slavery."

(254)

> "Hope" is the thing with feathers—
> That perches in the soul—
> And sings the tune without the words—
> And never stops—at all—
>
> And sweetest—in the Gale—is heard—
> And sore must be the storm—
> That could abash the little Bird
> That kept so many warm—
>
> I've heard it in the chillest land—
> And on the strangest Sea—
> Yet, never, in Extremity,
> It asked a crumb—of Me.
>
> *Emily Dickinson*

Advent is a season of hope. If we but open our souls to this singing bird and offer it gracious hospitality, we will indeed be blessed. But hope only comes when there is an atmosphere of faith. Belief in promises and presences creates an everlasting melody.

Hope, this ball of feathers, does not have easy sailing. Courage is necessary to confront the buffeting wings and waves of life. The paralytic had to have courage in the storms of his illness and even in the transforming encounter with Jesus. The synergism of both hope and courage led to new life.

Some winters are filled with discontent, some days so cold as to hold no promise of warmth. Yet God does not leave us without some comfort. Hope is a faithful bird that empowers us to face the future with determination and fortitude.

1. What is my Hope and what are my hopes?

2. What are some images of hope that enrich my journey of faith: Rainbow? Butterfly? Harvest? Kingdom?

3. What is the link between faith and hope for me?

Praying with the Church
    Lord,
    free us from our sins and make us whole.
    Hear our prayer,
    and prepare us to celebrate the incarnation of your Son,
    who lives and reigns with you and the Holy Spirit,
    one God, for ever and ever.

TUESDAY of the SECOND WEEK of ADVENT
Matthew 18:12–14

L ove does strange things. It is a grace filled with risks and is so desirous of unity that it takes supreme delight when oneness is restored. In God's love there is a preferential option for those who stray and there is grief because of their great need. Hopefully the ninety-nine will have enough love in their hearts to rejoice upon the finding of the one who was lost.

Refrain: "A voice is heard crying in the wilderness: Prepare the way of the Lord; make straight the path of our God."

(809)

Unable are the Loved to die
For Love is Immortality,
Nay, it is Deity—

Unable they that love—to die
For Love reforms Vitality
Into Divinity.

Emily Dickinson

Advent is a season of love. Our journey toward celebrating the birth of Christ is essentially an experience of God's love for us and for the world. As the days lose more and more of their light, we are given this light of grace, a light of love to counter the darkness and anxieties of life.

St. Augustine of Hippo describes grace in these terms: *"Quia amasti me, Domine, fecisti me amabilem."* ("Because you have loved me, O Lord, you have made me lovable.") There is herein a double blessing. God's love makes us lovable in an active sense, empowering us to love. And, in a passive sense, we are made capable of being loved.

Thus our immortality is assured with a double certitude. Those who are loved cannot die nor those who love cannot die because love is immortal, because love is God. As we begin thinking about gifts come Christmas day, we need not wait either to receive or give the one essential gift: love!

1.   From whom have I received "unconditional love"?

2.   What is the best way to package my love?

3.   How is love connected to advent faith and advent hope?

Praying with the Church
    Almighty God,
    help us to look forward
    to the glory of the birth of Christ our Savior:
    his coming is proclaimed joyfully
    to the ends of the earth,
    for he lives and reigns with you and the Holy Spirit,
    one God, for ever and ever.

WEDNESDAY of the SECOND WEEK of ADVENT
Matthew 11:28–30

In the Basilica of the National Shrine of the Immaculate Conception in Washington, D.C., there is a majestic bronze sculpture entitled "The Holy Family Resting—the Flight into Egypt" by artist Anna Hyatt Huntington. It is a sculpture depicting weariness and fatigue, as Mary, her infant Jesus, Joseph and their beast of burden sleep. This is the same child who, as a man, will tell people to share his yoke and who promises comfort. Meditating on this sculpture and the mystery of the flight into Egypt, we see our God-made-man take upon himself our human condition.

Refrain: "Zion, you will be renewed, and you will see the Just One who is coming to you."

(919)

> If I can stop one Heart from breaking
> I shall not live in vain
> If I can ease one Life the Aching
> Or cool one Pain
>
> Or help one fainting Robin
> Unto his Nest again
> I shall not live in Vain.

Emily Dickinson

Advent is a season of compassion. Our God comes to us again and again because our suffering and troubled lives are known in heaven. Nor is this coming an extrinsic approach. God comes in Jesus from the womb of Mary. This embrace of our human situation and this participation in our sorrows and joys are the result of divine compassion.

Compassion gives meaning to life. As we attempt to stop hearts from breaking, as we bring comfort to those in pain, as we express reverence toward all creation, we come to realize that our lives are not lived in vain. We take upon ourselves the yoke of others and find ourselves, perhaps for the first time, experiencing happiness.

Our Advent invitation is to come to the Lord who had to flee to Egypt, who knew the rigors of the desert, who took upon himself the yoke of the cross. From those difficult, painful experiences we have the assurance that our burdens are embraced by God's compassionate heart.

1. What Advent yoke can I take on myself?

2. What causes my degree of compassion to vary from person to person?

3. How is compassion linked to finding meaning in our lives?

Praying with the Church

All-powerful Father,
we await the healing power of Christ your Son.
Let us not be discouraged by our weaknesses
as we prepare for his coming.
Keep us steadfast in your love.
We ask this through our Lord Jesus Christ, your Son,
who lives and reigns with you and the Holy Spirit,
one God, for ever and ever.

THURSDAY of the SECOND WEEK of ADVENT
Matthew 11:11–15

One of the reasons why John the Baptist was so important in salvation history was because he was a truth-teller. The Baptist proclaimed Jesus as Messiah and called the people at the Jordan to repentance. More, John challenged Herod with the truth and was beheaded. Prophets pay a price for their truth-telling ministry—forfeiting acceptance by the establishment and often losing their lives. We must carefully "heed what you hear" for in the end the truth, and only the truth, will set us free.

Refrain: "The one who is coming after me existed before me; I am not worthy to untie his sandals."

(1129)

> Tell all the Truth but tell it slant—
> Success in Circuit lies
> Too bright for our infirm Delight
> The Truth's superb surprise
> As Lightning to the Children eased
> With explanation kind
> The Truth must dazzle gradually
> Or every man be blind—
>
> *Emily Dickinson*

Advent is a season of truth. In an age of relativism (à la Pilate's "What is truth?"), we find it difficult to listen to prophets who tell it the way it is: God's love for us, our sinfulness, restoration in Christ and in the Holy Spirit. We must keep returning to the double truth of our incredible dignity and our profound wretchedness caused by sin.

Truth is blinding, so we need to hear it and tell it in appropriate ways so as not to do harm. God "modifies" the truth so that we can take it in proper dosages. This is not to water down revelation but to respect the disposition of each listener. Just as children (and adults) are frightened by lightning and its associate thunder, we must comfort each other with gentle explanations.

Advent truth is indeed astounding: God with us in Jesus. But this "with-ness" involves believing that the infinite Deity has taken on our finite limitations. The Bethlehem mystery must be pondered in prayer if the truth is to be known. The "truth's superb surprise" brings deep joy to the believing heart.

1. Who are my truth-tellers?

2. Do I really seek the truth from others?

3. Why should some truths be told in the evening and not at the breakfast table?

Praying with the Church
Almighty Father,
give us the joy of your love
to prepare the way for Christ our Lord.
Help us to serve you and one another.
We ask this through our Lord Jesus Christ, your Son,
who lives and reigns with you and the Holy Spirit,
one God, for ever and ever.

FRIDAY of the SECOND WEEK of ADVENT
Matthew 11:16–19

"**Y**ou can't win!" "You're damned if you do; you're damned if you don't!" "They won't dance to a jig; they won't weep at a dirge!" We are all familiar with such situations in which certain individuals simply cannot be pleased. Jesus comes to celebrate with us and he is accused of being a glutton and drunkard. Jesus comes in fasting and the crowd thinks he is mad. Regardless of peoples' impressions, our Lord brought divine wisdom, which is to know what is truly pleasing to God. At times it is God's will that we weep in the face of suffering and sorrow; at times we are to celebrate the joys and holiness of life.

Refrain: "Rejoicing you shall draw water from the well-springs of the Savior."

(324)

Some keep the Sabbath going to Church—
I keep it, staying at Home—
With a Bobolink for a Chorister—
And an Orchard for a Dome—

Some keep the Sabbath in Surplice—
I just wear my Wings—
And instead of tolling the Bell for Church,
Our little Sexton—sings.

God preaches, a noted Clergyman—
And the sermon is never long,
So instead of getting to Heaven, at last—
I'm going, all along.

Emily Dickinson

Advent is a season of prayer. We are to give God quality time as we seek to deepen our bond of unity with our Creator. We need personal and public prayer; we need the quiet of the heart and the gathered assembly in worship. Thereby we are on our way to heaven.

God's preaching, whether long or short, is inclusive. At times the divine message is a call to freedom by way of discipline and fasting; at other times, we are to dance and sing for the glory of life. God longs that we be heavenbound, whatever our manner of celebrating the Sabbath.

Orchards and birds present us with nature's Sabbath. Organs and choirs link us to public worship on our Sunday Sabbaths. And whatever the melody, we know from whence all holiness comes and whither it leads. All copyright requests should be addressed: heaven!

1. Are my personal and public prayers integrated?

2. How do I keep the Sabbath?

3. Do I pray differently in the orchard than in a church?

Praying with the Church
    All-powerful God,
    help us to look forward in hope,
    to the coming of our Savior.
    May we live as he has taught,
    ready to welcome him with burning love and faith.
    We ask this through our Lord Jesus Christ, your Son,
    who lives and reigns with you and the Holy Spirit,
    one God, for ever and ever.

SATURDAY of the SECOND WEEK of ADVENT
Matthew 17:10–13

Elijah, John the Baptist, and the Son of Man shared something in common: their role of being prophets. This vocation involved speaking for God because it is the presence of the Spirit in the prophet which is moving and stirring the soul. Each of us is offered the gift of the Spirit and is invited into the ministry of Jesus through our baptism. As Jesus and the prophets of old worked at restoring all things to God, so each of us participates in this common endeavor. Empowered by the Spirit, we can accomplish this baptismal task.

Refrain: "There was no god before me and after me there will be none; every knee shall bend in worship, and every tongue shall praise me."

(674)

The Soul that hath a Guest
Doth seldom go abroad—
Diviner Crowd at Home—
Obliterate the need—

And Courtesy forbid
A Host's departure when
Upon Himself be visiting
The Emperor of Men—
Emily Dickinson

Advent is a season of courtesy. This is not a mere formal piece of etiquette but a graced reverence that bids us welcome the coming of grace. It is a hospitality that emerges from trust and deep love.

Our tradition keeps reminding us that we are "God's house." We have a divine Guest and that fact challenges us to stay at home from time to time. The divine Crowd—Father, Son, and Holy Spirit—has business to conduct with us. Busyness and schedules are no excuse for not tending to the home fires.

The inn had no room. Fair enough—first come, first served. But the inn of our souls is another matter. By grace, we are temples of God. By grace, we are hosts for the Emperor of men and women who need a Lord. Even Emily Post would agree that simple, basic, human courtesy forbids a host to vacate one's residence when entertaining a human guest, much less our God. Perhaps the best Christmas gift this year would be the pearl of courtesy.

1. What does courtesy imply?

2. Am I a good host to my dinner guests?

3. How many visitors have taken up permanent residence in my soul?

Praying with the Church
>Lord,
>let your glory dawn to take away our darkness.
>May we be revealed as the children of light
>at the coming of your Son,
>who lives and reigns with you and the Holy Spirit,
>one God, for ever and ever.

THIRD WEEK OF ADVENT

THIRD SUNDAY of ADVENT
Matthew 11:2–11 (A); John 1:6–8,19–28 (B), Luke 3:10–18 (C)

John the Baptist prepared the way for the Messiah. In the desert, at the Jordan, in prison, this prophet remained faithful to his vocation. None of us can know the extent of the temptations that bombarded his soul. We do know that he proclaimed and witnessed to Jesus and gave his life for the kingdom. This Advent prophet has a right to our attentiveness. More, this courageous disciple points us once again to the mystery of God's presence in Jesus.

Refrain: "Are you the One whose coming was foretold, or should we look for another? Tell John what you see: the blind have their sight restored, the dead are raised to life, the poor have the good news preached to them, alleluia."

> All of you undisturbed cities,
> haven't you ever longed for the Enemy?
> I'd like to see you besieged by him
> for ten endless and ground-shaking years.
>
> Until you were desperate and mad with suffering;
> finally in hunger you would feel his weight.

43

He lies outside the walls like a countryside.
And he knows very well how to endure
longer than the ones he comes to visit.

Climb up on your roofs and look out:
his camp is there, and his morale doesn't falter,
and his numbers do not decrease; he will not grow weaker,
and he sends no one into the city to threaten
or promise, and no one to negotiate.

He is the one who breaks down the walls,
and when he works, he works in silence.

Rainer Maria Rilke

Most of us prefer to live undisturbed lives. We strive to isolate ourselves from the fears of insecurity and the anxieties of poverty. By means of control and power we erect walls that protect us from the bruises of life. No "enemy," demon or divine, penetrates our fortified souls.

John the Baptist did not live such a life. God invaded his heart and turned him into a prophet. God besieged him day and night until all was surrendered to the divine will. No walls of separation remained to impede the currents of grace.

Advent is the coming of God into our planetary city. A disturbing enemy, indeed. God breaks down our walls of narcissism and greed until we are free to welcome the Lord of life and joy. It sometimes takes more than ten ground-shaking Advents to offer full hospitality.

1. How does God lay siege to my soul?

2. What are the walls that separate me from God's love and the love of people?

3. In what way does God come to me as the "Enemy"?

Praying with the Church

Father of our Lord Jesus Christ,
ever faithful to your promises,
and ever close to your Church:
the earth rejoices in hope of the Savior's coming
and looks forward with longing
to his return at the end of time.
Prepare our hearts and remove the sadness
that hinders us from feeling the joy
which his presence will bestow,
for he is Lord for ever and ever.

MONDAY of the THIRD WEEK of ADVENT
Matthew 21:23–27

Human curiosity is a powerful instinct. If curiosity can kill a cat, there is also a type of investigation that can bring us life. We long to know and to relate since we are made for truth and love. Yet the curiosity in the Gospel today—whether John's baptism was divine or human—is merely a guise to trip Jesus. The people coming to Jesus are not really interested in the life that flows from divine baptism but are worried about the authority of Jesus which threatens their own. Jesus, the true prophet, was not recognized because the people were not interested in truth but rather obsessed by the pleasure of power.

*Refrain: "All generations will call me blessed: the Lord has looked
with favor on his lowly servant."*

This is my labor—over it
my shadow lies like the shell of a nut.
It's true I'm the same as leaves and mud,
but as often as I pray or paint
it is Sunday, and in the valley I am
a jubilant Jerusalem.

I am the proud city of the Lord,
and praise him with a hundred tongues;
David's thanks have found a resonance in me;
I lay in the twilight of harps
and breathed in the evening star.

My streets rise toward sunrise.
After people have left me alone a long time
it happens that I am larger.
Inside me I hear steps ring
and I stretch my loneliness out
from eternity to eternity.

Rainer Maria Rilke

The labor of Jesus was one of life. His work, like that of the
Baptist, was to call people to achieve their full human dignity,
to one day be citizens of a jubilant Jerusalem. Jesus' work was
one of salvation.

Instead of being people of praise and theology for all that
God was doing in their lives, the elders and authorities chose
the route of argumentation and power. Jesus and John threat-
ened their understanding of existence. No longer could these
power-brokers hear the music of the harps nor see the glory
of the night sky.

Jesus knew loneliness, the loneliness that comes in not being understood. Ultimately it would come down to the loneliness of Calvary. Yet Jesus refused to withdraw into solitude. He came that he might make Jerusalem a jubilant city. That was his labor of love.

1. What is my life's work, my labor?

2. Am I more comfortable with logic or thanksgiving?

3. Why am I sometimes lonely?

Praying with the Church
   Lord,
   hear our voices raised in prayer.
   Let the light of the coming of your Son
   free us from the darkness of sin.
   We ask this through our Lord Jesus Christ, your Son,
   who lives and reigns with you and the Holy Spirit,
   one God, for ever and ever.

TUESDAY of the THIRD WEEK of ADVENT
Matthew 21: 28–32

The test of discipleship, the following of Jesus, is more a matter of deeds than words. We might give verbal consent to God's commands but the test will be in the living (orthopraxis). God asks us to work in the vineyard so that there might be an abundant harvest. The kingdom comes when we are just, loving, and people of faith. Repentance and belief is a matter of action. Here is the way of holiness that John preached and that many of the marginal people in society listened to and put into practice.

Refrain: "*Before Mary and Joseph had come together, they learned that Mary was with child by the power of the Holy Spirit, alleluia.*"

I have faith in all those things that are not yet said.
I want to set free my most holy feelings.
What no one has dared to want
will be for me impossible to refuse.

If that is presumption, then, my God, forgive me.
However, I want to tell you this one thing:
I want my best strength to be like a shoot,
with no anger and no timidity, as a shoot is;
this is the way the children love you.

With these ebbing tides, with these mouths
opening their deltas into the open sea,
with these returns, that keep growing,
I want to acknowledge you, I want to announce you,
as no one ever has before.

And if that is arrogance, then I will stay arrogant
for the sake of my prayer,
that is so sincere and solitary
standing before your cloudy forehead.

Rainer Maria Rilke

Faith is at the center of our Advent season. Some people believed in the preaching of John the Baptist and entered the land of holiness. Some believed in the preaching of Jesus and discovered peace and the kingdom of God. Faith is that truthful reliance in God's liberating love and forgiveness. Faith may even lead to a holy presumption and a healthy arrogance because we realize that all life and holiness come from God.

Advent is a time to acknowledge and announce the good news of God's love made present and manifest in Jesus. It is also a season of sincere and solitary prayer, a communication with God that leads to communion.

Those who believe and repent, like the tax collector and prostitute mentioned in today's Gospel, gain a new freedom. We can hear their heart's cry: "I came to set free my most holy feelings." Through Jesus' redemptive love, there is no need to return to feelings of greed and lust which only result in anger and timidity.

1. How has my faith grown since the start of Advent?

2. What are some of my most holy feelings?

3. When has my faith led me to repentance?

Praying with the Church

Father of love,
you made a new creation
through Jesus Christ your Son.
May his coming free us from sin
and renew his life within us,
for he lives and reigns with you and the Holy Spirit,
one God, for ever and ever.

WEDNESDAY of the THIRD WEEK of ADVENT
Luke 7: 18–23

Stumbling blocks keep us from reaching our goal. Jesus was aware that people had different expectations of the coming Messiah. Some were looking for a strong political savior who would overthrow foreign power and give the nation social and economic freedom. When Jesus was about the ministry of healing, preaching, and restoring life, many walked away because they were looking for a different Messiah. Even John the Baptist was perplexed and we wonder if perhaps he too was hoping for something more.

Refrain: "You, O Lord, are the One whose coming was foretold: we long for you to come and set your people free."

> I can tell by the way the trees beat, after
> so many dull days, on my worried windowpanes
> that a storm is coming,
> and I hear the far-off fields say things
> I can't bear without a friend,
> I can't love without a sister.
>
> The storm, the shifter of shapes, drives on
> across the woods and across time,
> and the world looks as if it had no age:
> the landscape, like a line in the psalm book,
> is seriousness and weight and eternity.
>
> What we choose to fight is so tiny!
> What fights with us is so great!
> If only we would let ourselves be dominated

as things do by some immense storm,
we would become strong too, and not need names.

When we win it's with small things,
and the triumph itself makes us small.
What is extraordinary and eternal
does not *want* to be bent by us.
I mean the Angel who appeared
to the wrestlers of the Old Testament:
when the wrestlers' sinews
grew long like metal strings,
he felt them under his fingers
like chords of deep music.

Whoever was beaten by this Angel
(who often simply declined the fight)
went away proud and strengthened
and great from that harsh hand,
that kneaded him as if to change his shape.
Winning does not tempt that man.
This is how he grows: by being defeated, decisively,
by constantly greater beings.

Rainer Maria Rilke

One of the stumbling blocks in life is winning and success.
Our victories, so often tiny and insignificant, give us a false
sense of power and prestige. Little do we realize that every
feather we add to our bonnet has to be plucked out before
entering God's kingdom.

Again we come across the Christian paradox: being defeated
decisively may well be our ultimate victory. Just ask Jacob who
wrestled all night with the Angel. What would have happened
had he won? His limp would forever be a sign of far-off things.

Jesus seems to have lost! He came to bring life but was nailed to a tree. An apparent decisive defeat and this a stumbling block to those expecting a human victory. "He saved us, let him save himself"—and many stumbled as they left the hill of Calvary.

1. What do I expect of the Messiah?

2. Can I name three stumbling blocks on my journey!

3. What are my expectations of Jesus and the Church?

Praying with the Church

Father,
may the coming celebration of the birth of your Son
bring us your saving help
and prepare us for eternal life.
Grant this through our Lord Jesus Christ, your Son,
who lives and reigns with you and the Holy Spirit,
one God, for ever and ever.

OCTAVE BEFORE CHRISTMAS

FOURTH SUNDAY of ADVENT
Matthew 1:1–18 (A); Luke 1:26–38 (B); Luke 1:39–45 (C)

Allll kinds of "advents" happen in life: the coming of angels and dawns, the coming of visitors with good and bad news, the coming of joys and sorrows. Human life does not stand still and we, who often desire permanence and stability, must deal with the constant flow of time and events. Joseph, Mary, and Elizabeth are fellow pilgrims who, although caught up in the historical process of life, were grounded and centered in the mystery of love. Theirs is a song that goes on and on and on in great beauty and joy.

Refrain: (See the refrain from the specific day of December that the Fourth Sunday falls on.)

My life is not this steeply sloping hour,
in which you see me hurrying.
Much stands behind me: I stand before it like a tree;
I am only one of my many mouths,
and at that, the one that will be still the soonest.

I am the rest between two notes,
which are somehow always in discord
because Death's note wants to climb over—

but in the dark interval, reconciled,
they stay there trembling.
And the song goes on, beautiful.

Rainer Maria Rilke

Our Christian lives involve urgency and rest. We hurry about attempting to meet the many demands of living: doing laundry, preparing meals, paying bills, going to a movie. But our lives are so much more than this frenetic activity. These duties and times of leisure are only one dimension of our complex lives.

We live between the past and the future, between memories and dreams. It is in the present moment of grace—be it an angel's voice, the cry of the poor, the whisper to kneel and pray—that we take responsibility for our tiny lives. We live in a constant flux between death and resurrection.

Deep faith assures us that in this process of dying and rising a song of great beauty and fidelity continues to be sung. It is the song of love, the Advent song. It is the melody that God is with us.

1. What is the pace of my life?

2. How do my memories and dreams relate to the kingdom of God?

3. What is the theme song of my spiritual life?

Praying with the Church

Father, all-powerful God,
your eternal Word took flesh on our earth
when the Virgin Mary placed her life
at the service of your plan.
Lift our minds in watchful hope
to hear the voice which announces his glory

and open our minds to receive the Spirit
who prepares us for his coming.
We ask this through Christ our Lord.

WEEKDAY in the OCTAVE before CHRISTMAS
December 17
Matthew 1:1–17

Genealogies are about genes, those microscopic "things" that carry our history into every inch of our being. Jesus' genealogy (and his genes) contained some interesting ancestry. There was Abraham's faith; David's adultery and murder and repentant psalms; Solomon's wisdom and political intrigue. As we near the Nativity of the Lord, we are reminded from whence our Messiah came, we are invited to ponder our own genealogy all the way back to our God who has planted the genes of grace in our souls.

Refrain: "Wisdom, O holy Word of God, you govern all creation with your strong yet tender care. Come and show your people the way to salvation."

MY-NESS

"My parents, my husband, my brother, my sister."
I am listening in a cafeteria at breakfast.

> The women's voices rustle, fulfill themselves
> In a ritual no doubt necessary.
> I glance sidelong at their moving lips
> And I delight in being here on earth
> For one more moment, with them, here on earth,
> To celebrate our tiny, tiny my-ness.
>
> *Czeslaw Milosz*

Jesus had a long ancestry of my-ness: my mother, my tribes, my God. Though the history was clouded with deceit and war, it was also filled with joys and goodness. Jesus entered fully into the human condition and tasted our poverty and riches.

Though the path he trod was difficult, Jesus delighted "in being here on earth." Just as the Father delighted in the sons and daughters of earth, Jesus too took joy in being part of the human family. That delight and joy flooded from a heart of love and the longing to lead all people back to the Father.

In Advent we celebrate the mystery of Jesus. But his tiny my-ness is large with meaning: my mother who did whatever God asked of her; my cousin John who called people to repent and believe; my disciples who left everything to follow me. Not so tiny, these treasured possessions.

1. What "my-ness" is uniquely my own?

2. How do I celebrate the people and things God has given me?

3. Let me list and then delight in my personal genealogy.

Praying with the Church
   Father,
   Creator and Redeemer of mankind,

you decreed, and your Word became man,
born of the Virgin Mary.
May we come to share the divinity of Christ,
who humbled himself to share in our human nature,
for he lives and reigns with you and the Holy Spirit,
one God, for ever and ever.

WEEKDAY in the OCTAVE before CHRISTMAS
December 18
Matthew 1:18–24

When the angel of the Lord appeared to Mary at the time of the Annunciation the message was, "Have no fear." When Joseph pondered what to do when he discovered that Mary was with child the angel proclaimed, "Have no fear." The Advent message is clear: God is with us, the Holy Spirit overshadows us, Jesus comes to save his people from sin. Our Trinitarian spirituality is the basis for our courage. We, like Mary and Joseph, need not be afraid because of one word, one mystery: Emmanuel.

Refrain: "O sacred Lord of ancient Israel, who showed yourself to Moses in the burning bush, who gave him the holy law on Sinai mountain: come, stretch out your mighty hand to set us free."

VENI CREATOR

Come, Holy Spirit,
bending or not bending the grasses,
appearing or not above our heads in a tongue of flame,
at hay harvest or when they plough in the orchards or
    when snow
covers crippled firs in the Sierra Nevada.
I am only a man: I need visible signs.
I tire easily, building the stairway of abstraction.
Many a time I asked, you know it well, that the statue in church
lift its hand, only once, just once, for me.
But I understand that signs must be human,
therefore call one man, anywhere on earth,
not me—after all I have some decency—
and allow me, when I look at him, to marvel at you.

Czeslaw Milosz

Advent holds a paradox. We look forward to the coming of
the Christ child who has already come. We desire God's
coming who has always been here. We pray "Come, Holy
Spirit," a Spirit that continually broods over our bent and
fragile would.

We do that because we keep absenting ourselves from
God's presence. We seek visible signs because our faith is weak
and we need tangible assurances of divine providence. We
grow weary easily, we become fearful at the first sign of darkness, we construct abstractions to escape the specific requests
of God.

When the Holy Spirit comes we experience a love that
drives out fear. There are certain individuals—saints and
prophets and parents and teachers—who say yes to the

coming Spirit. We marvel in their presence at their gentleness, goodness and graciousness.

1. Who are some people in my life who witness to the Holy Spirit?

2. How often do I pray from the heart: "Come, Holy Spirit"?

3. Why does love drive out fear?

Praying with the Church
All-powerful God,
renew us by the coming feast of your Son
and free us from our slavery to sin.
Grant this through our Lord Jesus Christ, your Son,
who lives and reigns with you and the Holy Spirit,
one God, for ever and ever.

WEEKDAY in the OCTAVE before CHRISTMAS
December 19
Luke 1:5–25

Zechariah and Mary had a shared experience. Appearance of an angel, fear, not knowing how a child would or could be born. There was one major difference. Mary trusted in the words spoken to her by God's messenger whereas

Zechariah did not. The consequences we know: Mary gives birth to the Word; Zechariah is struck mute until his son is born.

Refrain: "O Flower of Jesse's stem, you have been raised up as a sign for all peoples; kings stand silent in your presence; the nations bow down in worship before you. Come, let nothing keep you from coming to our aid."

SECRETARIES

I am no more than a secretary of the invisible thing
That is dictated to me and a few others.
Secretaries, mutually unknown, we walk the earth
Without much comprehension. Beginning a phrase in the
     middle
Or ending it with a comma. And how it all looks when
     completed
Is not up to us to inquire, we won't read it anyway.

                                        Czeslaw Milosz

God is dictating constantly. Mary listened and, good secretary and maidservant that she was, wrote out in her life God's invisible plan. Jesus was the word spoken, conceived and born in history through Mary.

Zechariah had more difficulty in fulfilling his task as secretary to the things of God. He found the word spoken almost impossible, given the limits of age. In the middle of the sentence he fell mute. It wasn't until John's birth that he regained his faith and began to comprehend. A fraction of the mystery.

God speaks to us during this season of Advent. As good secretaries we are to listen attentively and record in our hearts the message of God's newness. More is required. We are to live the words of the gospel like Mary did. Though we never fully comprehend the message, faith supports us on our way.

1. Do I consider myself a good secretary of God's word?

2. What specific messages has God dictated to me?

3. List two or three good secretaries of God's invisible things.

Praying with the Church
Father,
you show the world the splendor of your glory
in the coming of Christ, born of the Virgin.
Give to us true faith and love
to celebrate the mystery of God made man.
We ask this through our Lord Jesus Christ, your Son,
who lives and reigns with you and the Holy Spirit,
one God, for ever and ever.

WEEKDAY in the OCTAVE before CHRISTMAS
December 20
Luke 1:26–38

Mary found favor with God. Herein is the source of her joy and her mission in life. This highly favored daughter was to conceive, bear and raise a son. Though deeply troubled by this event, and not comprehending all the details, Mary identifies herself as the maidservant of God. Her will gave way to God's design. We cannot celebrate the Nativity without pondering the mystery of the Annunciation. Indeed, "nothing is impossible with God."

Refrain: "O Key of David, O royal Power of Israel controlling at your will the gate of heaven; come, break down the prison walls of death for those who dwell in darkness and the shadow of death and lead your captive people into freedom."

AN HOUR

Leaves glowing in the sun, zealous hum of bumblebees,
From afar, from somewhere beyond the river, echoes of
    lingering voices
And the unhurried sounds of a hammer gave joy not only
    to me.
Before the five senses were opened, and earlier than any
    beginning
They waited, ready, for all those who would call
    themselves mortals,
So that they might praise, as I do, life, that is, happiness.

Czeslaw Milosz

How many times Mary must have pondered "her hour" when God broke into her life to ask her to be the mother of Jesus. No glowing leaves, perhaps, no bumblebees humming, no hammer's unhurried sound. But surely a lingering voice of an angel speaking of trust and the overshadowing Spirit.

All of Mary's senses were open, inner and outer. Her attentiveness was supreme and her willingness absolute. Here we see the obedient one, the one who listened in love and cried "yes"!

There is cause here for praise and happiness because life is being lived to the full. In John's Gospel we read that Jesus came to bring life, full, abundant life (John 10:10) and we see this mission already being realized in Mary.

1. How alive and open are my senses: seeing, hearing, tasting, smelling, touching?

2. What are my "special hours" when leaves glow, bees hum, voices echo?

3. Is happiness the same as obedience?

Praying with the Church
> God of love and mercy,
> help us to follow the example of Mary,
> always ready to do your will.
> At the message of an angel
> she welcomed your eternal Son
> and, filled with the light of your Spirit,
> she became the temple of your Word,
> who lives and reigns with you and the Holy Spirit,
> one God, for ever and ever.

WEEKDAY in the OCTAVE before CHRISTMAS
December 21
Luke 1:39–45

Good news must be shared. When one is given new life, one looks for a rooftop or a mountain from which to shout out the joy. Mary and Elizabeth were chosen as vital instruments in the work of salvation. They would give birth to two prophets: Jesus and the Baptist. If we read the word of God with deep faith, we realize that we too are part of this story. Our call is to trust that God's word of love and forgiveness will be fulfilled in our lives.

Refrain: "O Radiant Dawn, splendor of eternal light, sun of justice: come, shine on those who dwell in darkness and the shadow of death."

THANKFULNESS

You gave me gifts, God-Enchanter.
I give you thanks for good and ill.
Eternal light in everything on earth.
As now, so on the day after my death.

Czeslaw Milosz

God is a giver of gifts. For Mary and Elizabeth that was the gift of new life. For each of us the gift of time, the gift of freedom and opportunity, the gift of grace. An Advent challenge: take nothing for granted. We, who live in radical indigence, have been dearly and abundantly blessed.

Reception of gifts is not enough. We must give thanks; we must become an enchanted people. Thankfulness comes in two forms: words of gratitude and gifts shared joyfully and with charity. A test will always be the ability to give thanks for both good and difficult experiences.

Beneath thankfulness lies faith. We believe, as Mary and Elizabeth, that an eternal light illumines all creation and that even death cannot extinguish the flame. Here is a deep gratitude that leads to peace.

1. What gifts has God given to me this Advent?

2. What gifts have I given to God?

3. How is thankfulness linked to thoughtfulness?

Praying with the Church
Lord,
hear the prayers of your people.
May we who celebrate the birth of your Son as man
rejoice in the gift of eternal life when he comes in glory,
for he lives and reigns with you and the Holy Spirit,
one God, for ever and ever.

WEEKDAY in the OCTAVE before CHRISTMAS
December 22
Luke 1:46–56

Mary sang the praises of the Lord for many reasons. First of all, God looked upon her in her lowliness and poverty. And, as St. John of the Cross reminds us, where God looks, God loves. Second, Mary's song proclaimed how merciful God is to those who fear him. In Jesus that mercy would take on supreme visibility. Thirdly, God demonstrates divine power by raising the lowly and feeding those who are hungry. Mary sang because God is faithful to all the promises of old.

Refrain: "O King of all the nations, the only joy of every human heart; O Keystone of the mighty arch of man, come and save the creature you fashioned from the dust."

INCANTATION

Human reason is beautiful and invincible.
No bars, no barbed wire, no pulping of books,
No sentence of banishment can prevail against it.
It establishes the universal ideas in language,
And guides our hand so we write Truth and Justice
With capital letters, lie and oppression with small.
It puts what should be above things as they are,
Is an enemy of despair and a friend of hope.
It does not know Jew from Greek or slave from master,
Giving us the estate of the world to manage.
It saves austere and transparent phrases
From the filthy discord of tortured words.

It says that everything is new under the sun,
Opens the congealed fist of the past.
Beautiful and very young are Philo-Sophia
And poetry, her ally in the service of the good.
As late as yesterday Nature celebrated their birth,
The news was brought to the mountains by a unicorn and
an echo.
Their friendship will be glorious, their time has no limit.
Their enemies have delivered themselves to destruction.

Czeslaw Milosz

Here is a song to human reason and wisdom, two gifts that enrich and enlarge our lives. Reason, well-ordered, guides us toward truth and justice, healing the world and bringing about a certain degree of peace.

But Mary's song goes beyond reason in the poetry of faith. In this land it is love that is experienced and responded to. Far more beautiful than reason, far younger than wisdom, love is the greatest of all gifts. Her presence leads to joy and peace.

Mary brings us good news not of some mythical unicorn but of God's favor. Someone once said that joy is the echo of God's love. Mary's incantation does echo down the centuries and calls us to join her in her majestic Magnificat.

1. What weight do I assign to reason, to love?

2. Can I write my own "Magnificat"?

3. Why is love beautiful and invincible?

Praying with the Church
God our Father,
you sent your Son
to free mankind from the power of death.

May we who celebrate the coming of Christ as man
share more fully in his divine life,
for he lives and reigns with you and the Holy Spirit,
one God, for ever and ever.

WEEKDAY in the OCTAVE before CHRISTMAS
December 23
Luke 1:55–66

Two days before Christmas we are invited to another nativity and naming: the birth of John the Baptist. This event was accompanied by an unusual happening that caused fear and amazement. John's father Zechariah was given his speech back. He who doubted and became mute now believed and praised God. What all this meant was not clear except for one thing: the hand of the Lord continued to shape salvation history. This child, the Baptist, would prepare the way of the Messiah.

Refrain: "O Emmanuel, king and lawgiver, desire of the nations, Savior of all people, come and set us free, Lord our God."

FAITH

Faith is in you whenever you look
At a dewdrop or a floating leaf

And know that they are because they have to be.
Even if you close your eyes and dream up things
The world will remain as it has always been
And the leaf will be carried by the waters of the river.
You have faith also when you hurt your foot
Against a sharp rock and you know
That rocks are here to hurt our feet.
See the long shadow that is cast by the tree?
We and the flowers throw shadows on the earth.
What has no shadow has no strength to live.

Czeslaw Milosz

Faith fluctuated in the heart of Zechariah. God's word to him was questioned to such an extent that it took his voice away. But now, seeing the birth of his son, his faith returned and with it the capacity to communicate once again.

What Zechariah now saw, whether a dewdrop or leaf or infant's face, deepened his conviction of God's abiding presence and awesome providence. Even when suffering would come, sharp rocks bruising his feet or a son thrown into jail, Zechariah had his faith to support and heal him.

Down through the ages we see Zechariah's double shadow: his initial doubt and his restored faith. His was a human journey that most of us can identify with. This Advent season is yet another invitation to cast our shadow of faith upon the road of life.

1. What are the elements of life that nurture my faith?

2. How does my faith deal with the hurts and sufferings of life?

3. What type of shadow does my faith cast?

Praying with the Church
> Father, we contemplate the birth of your Son.
> He was born of the Virgin Mary
> and came to live among us.
> May we receive forgiveness and mercy
> through our Lord Jesus Christ, your Son,
> who lives and reigns with you and the Holy Spirit,
> one God, for ever and ever.

WEEKDAY in the OCTAVE before CHRISTMAS
December 24
Luke 1:67–79

Now it is Zechariah's turn to sing. His canticle rings down the ages with the good news of salvation. Not only was Zechariah's tongue freed, but his soul was enlightened to understand that in Jesus, God's promises of mercy would come to fruition and in his son, John, we would be told salvation comes through freedom from our sins. This freedom is rooted in the kindness and compassion of our God who visits us in the Word-made-flesh.

Refrain: "When the sun rises in the morning sky, you will see the King of kings coming forth from the Father like a radiant bridegroom from the bridal chamber."

GIFT

A day so happy.
Fog lifted early, I worked in the garden.
Hummingbirds were stopping over honeysuckle flowers.
There was no thing on earth I wanted to possess.
I knew no one worth my envying him.
Whatever evil I suffered, I forgot.
To think that once I was the same man did not embarrass me.
In my body I felt no pain.
When straightening up, I saw the blue sea and sails.

Czeslaw Milosz

Zechariah could identify with this poem. He knew himself to be gifted and his happiness broke into song. His son John would play an instrumental role in the plan of salvation. The Holy Spirit enlightened this aged man to see the tender compassion of God.

No acquisitiveness nor envy could ever touch Zechariah's soul. A new freedom through new knowledge was given to him. Indeed, the song here sung arises for a saved man. Even the suffering and embarrassment that led to his deafness was now behind him.

Old age brings pain and often discouragement. But when one's life is filled with grace the pain is somehow transformed and one's view is enlarged to see distant things with clarity and hope. The gift given to Zechariah is our own in his beautiful canticle.

1. What moment of grace leads me to sing?

2. Are there things I long to possess: people I envy?

3.   How do I deal with pain and embarrassment?

Praying with the Church
Come, Lord Jesus,
do not delay;
give new courage to your people who trust in your love.
By your coming, raise us to the joy of your kingdom,
where you live and reign with the Father and the Holy Spirit,
one God, for ever and ever.

CHRISTMAS

FIRST DAY in the OCTAVE of CHRISTMAS
December 25
Luke 2:1–14

Today when a child is born, video cameras are often used to record many of the proceedings: the wait in the delivery room, the wrinkled skin of the newborn, the parents holding gently their new life. We have no video of the birth of Jesus. But we do have some aspects of the event: shepherds and angels, hosannas and fear, poverty and wonderment. At the center is the mystery of faith: God enters history. Jesus, the Word-made-flesh, is born of Mary. Night would no longer be dark because of a new Light. Night would not ever be silent again because of good news that must be shouted and proclaimed.

Refrain: "Christ the Lord is born today; today, the Savior has appeared. Earth echoes songs of angel choirs, archangels' joyful praise. Today on earth his friends exult: Glory to God in the highest, alleluia."

ON ANGELS

All was taken away from you: white dresses,
wings, even existence.
Yet I believe you,
messengers.

73

There, where the world is turned inside out,
a heavy fabric embroidered with stars and beasts,
you stroll, inspecting the trustworthy seams.

Short is your stay here:
now and then at a matinal hour, if the sky is clear,
in a melody repeated by a bird,
or in the smell of apples at the close of day
when the light makes the orchards magic.

They say somebody has invented you
but to me this does not sound convincing
for humans invented themselves as well.

The voice — no doubt it is a valid proof,
as it can belong only to radiant creatures,
weightless and winged (after all, why not?),
girdled with the lightning.

I have heard that voice many a time when asleep
and, what is strange, I understood more or less
an order or an appeal in an unearthly tongue:
day draws near
another one
do what you can.

Czeslaw Milosz

We too believe in the message of the angels. Our faith rests on
the infant child born in poverty to save the world. The angels'
song awakes us to be attentive to God's visitation. That
melody is continually repeated Advent after Advent.

Certain voices still tell of God-with-us: the voice of
teachers sharing the truths of our faith; the voice of prophets
calling us to justice that is part of God's kingdom; the voice
and works of artists who incarnate God's beauty. These

messengers are not weightless nor are they winged. But they are sent from God, and like Jesus, bring light to our darkness.

The day draws near. The Christmas mystery is upon us. We must do what God has empowered us to do: enflesh love in deeds of kindness.

1. Over the years who have been the messengers that communicate daily the Christmas event to me?

2. What is the most important thing we can do on Christmas day?

3. To whom has my voice brought a message of love?

Praying with the Church

    Almighty God and Father of light,
    a child is born for us and a son is given to us.
    Your eternal Word leaped down from heaven
    in the silent watches of the night,
    and now your Church is filled with wonder
    at the nearness of her God.
    Open our hearts to receive his life
    and increase our vision with the rising dawn,
    that our lives may be filled with his glory and his peace,
    who lives and reigns for ever and ever.

CHRISTMASTIDE

SECOND DAY in the OCTAVE of CHRISTMAS
December 26: Stephen, First Martyr
Matthew 10:17–22

Birth one day, death the next. There is no respite from Christian realism. We are born to die. We come from God and return again to our Creator, our work having been done. Like Jesus, Stephen was handed over. Stephen was given the words to say, words of evangelization as he crossed the threshold of death: "Look! I see an opening in the sky, and the Son of Man standing at God's right hand." Jesus, the babe became savior, received Stephen's spirit.

Refrain: "While earth was rapt in silence and night only half through its course, your almighty Word, O Lord, came down from his royal throne, alleluia."

THE WINDOWS

Lord, how can man preach thy eternal word?
 He is a brittle crazy glass:
Yet in thy temple thou dost him afford
  This glorious and transcendent place,
  To be a window, through thy grace.

But when thou dost anneal in glass thy story,
   Making thy life to shine within
The holy Preacher's; then the light and glory
   More rev'rend grows, and more doth win:
   Which else shows wat'rish, bleak, and thin.

Doctrine and life, colours and light, in one
   When they combine and mingle, bring
A strong regard and awe: but speech alone
   Doth vanish like a flaring thing,
   And in the ear, not conscience ring.

George Herbert

Stephen gave a short sermon but it has been long remembered throughout Christian history. His "glorious and transcendent place" was martyrdom but no stones thrown at him could break the luminous windows of his soul. His life brought light and glory just as his words pierced the conscience of those who took his life.

Someone stood by when Stephen was murdered: a man named Saul. Could the thorn in the flesh that Saul (later Paul) suffered have been this event? No matter. Paul would one day follow Stephen who followed Jesus into his own flogging and death. Another window of God's grace that continues to commingle doctrine and life, real colors and unforgettable light.

1. What were some moments in my life when I felt a window of God's grace?

2. Why does the Church celebrate a martyrdom the day after the savior's birth?

3. What stained glass window best tells the story of God's love for me and the world?

Praying with the Church:

> All powerful God,
> may the human birth of your Son
> free us from our former slavery to sin
> and bring us new life.
> We ask this through our Lord Jesus Christ, your Son,
> who lives and reigns with you and the Holy Spirit,
> one God, for ever and ever.

THIRD DAY in the OCTAVE of CHRISTMAS
December 27: John, Apostle and Evangelist
John 20:2–8

Yesterday, on the feast of the first martyr Stephen, the Church linked together birth and death. Now, two days after Christmas, we link the birth of Christ with a resurrection story. Peter and John run to the empty tomb. John outruns his cohort, waits for Simon Peter to enter first, then goes in and has a faith experience. Suddenly sad, sorrowing hearts awake and arise. The new day of faith has dawned.

Refrain: "Virgin Mary, all that the prophets foretold of Christ has been fulfilled through you: as a virgin you conceived, and after you gave birth, a virgin you remained."

THE DAWNING

Awake sad heart, whom sorrow ever drowns;
 Take up thine eyes, which feed on earth;
Unfold thy forehead gather'd into frowns:
 Thy Savior comes, and with him mirth:
  Awake, awake;
And with a thankful heart his comforts take.
 But thou dost still lament, and pine, and cry;
 And feel his death, but not his victory.

Arise sad heart; if thou dost not withstand,
 Christ's resurrection thine may be:
Do not be hanging down break from the hand,
 Which as it riseth, raiseth thee:
  Arise, arise;
And with his burial-linen dry thine eyes:
 Christ left his grave-clothes, that we might, when grief
 Draws tears, or blood, not want an handkerchief.

         George Herbert

The Gospel does not indicate whether or not Simon Peter and John possessed handkerchiefs. No cause for concern. In the empty tomb there were wrappings of pieces of cloth rolled up in a place by themselves. A thoughtful God helping us to deal with the tears and blood of our grief, with the tears and juices of our joys.

One can imagine the sad and sorrowing hearts of the disciples. Their Lord and Master slain. But now new life, now it is that the resurrection awakens faith and causes their sad hearts to rise with new courage. In their joy did they perhaps press the burial linens to their lips and use them to dry their eyes?

1.   What do I use to deal with my griefs and tears?

2.   Why do we so easily feel death and not Christ's victory? Do we need a heart transplant?

3.   Read the Prologue of John's Gospel—a real dawning!

Praying with the Church:
Father,
we are filled with the new light
by the coming of your Word among us.
May the light of faith
shine in our words and actions.

We ask this through our Lord Jesus Christ, your Son,
who lives and reigns with you and the Holy Spirit,
one God, for ever and ever.

FOURTH DAY in the OCTAVE of CHRISTMAS
December 28: Holy Innocents, Martyrs
Matthew 2:13–18

The world was shocked when a gunman broke into a school room in Scotland and shot a teacher and over a dozen of her small children. A massacre which has left the people in Scotland traumatized. A cry can still be heard in the Scottish hills, loud lamentation and sobbing. Innocent life so cruelly cut short leaving the world shaken.

Refrain: "*The Holy Virgin gave birth to God who became for us the frail, tender baby she nursed at her breast. Let us worship the Lord who comes to save us.*"

THE AGONY

Philosophers have measur'd mountains,
Fathom'd the depths of seas, of states, and kings,
Walk'd with a staff to heav'n, and traced fountains:
　　But there are two vast, spacious things,
The which to measure it doth more behove:
Yet few there are that sound them; Sin and Love.

Who would know Sin, let him repair
Unto Mount Olivet; there shall he see
A man so wrung with pains, that all his hair,
　　His skin, his garments bloody be.
Sin is that press and vice, which forceth pain
To hunt his cruel food through ev'ry vein.

Who knows not Love, let him assay
And taste that juice, which on the cross a pike
Did set again abroach, then let him say
　　If ever he did taste the like.
Love is that liquor sweet and most divine,
Which my God feels as blood; but I, as wine.

George Herbert

Herod sinned, slaughtering the Holy Innocents. No philosophy can sound the depths of sin and agony. But we do have some knowledge of sin, some expression of agony. We join Jesus in Gethsemane and there see our innocent Lord bathed in blood. We see what sin has done.

Jesus loved us unto death, death on a cross. Again no philosophy has succeeded in defining love but we can taste this sweet liquor. Its intoxicating power (*in vino veritas*) sets us free. The only way to deal with the agony of the Holy Innocents is to discover the meaning of sin and love in the paschal mystery.

1. What is my understanding of sin and love?

2. How do I protect innocent life?

3. Where does Rachel bewail her children today?

Praying with the Church
Lord God,
we praise you for creating man,
and still more for restoring him in Christ.
Your Son shared our weakness:
may we share his glory,
for he lives and reigns with you and the Holy Spirit,
one God, for ever and ever.

FIFTH DAY in the OCTAVE of CHRISTMAS
December 29
Luke 2:22–35

What is the first and last lie we tell ourselves? "It's mine!" All is a gift and Jesus was brought to the temple in that spirit. As the first-born male he was consecrated to the Lord. Simeon was there to confirm the dedication. In Jesus all people would experience light and glory even though suffering and contradiction would be part of the mix. No lies here. Just the glorious truth of God's love.

Refrain: "The King of heaven humbled himself to be born of a virgin, that he might restore man to the kingdom he had lost."

THE DEDICATION

Lord, my first fruits present themselves to thee;
Yet not mine neither: for from thee they came,
And must return. Accept of them and me,
And make us strive, who shall sing best thy name.
Turn their eyes hither, who shall make a gain;
Theirs, who shall hurt themselves for me, refrain.

George Herbert

The Lord has blessed each one of us abundantly. What return shall we make? Good disciples/stewards offer first fruits, not leftovers. Through baptism we dedicate our lives to a God who has consecrated himself to us.

Simeon's song is well sung. Indeed, he should be nominated for this one "who shall sing best thy name." As the "revealing light to the Gentiles, the glory of your people

Israel," we have the lyrics of a dream song. Maybe the best fruit we can offer God is a life that is a song of love. This is full, complete dedication.

1. Memorize Simeon's song and use it as a night prayer.

2. Since Christmas, what gifts of time, talent and treasure have I given to the Lord?

3. How is it helpful to dedicate each day to a specific intention?

Praying with the Church
All powerful and unseen God,
the coming of your light into our world
has made the darkness vanish.
Teach us to proclaim the birth of your Son Jesus Christ,
who lives and reigns with you and the Holy Spirit,
one God, forever and ever.

SIXTH DAY in the OCTAVE of CHRISTMAS
December 30
Luke 2:36–40

Anna, the prophetess, was a grateful woman. Not only was she graced with a long life and deep faith but, in her old age, she saw the deliverance of Israel in the infant

Jesus. Her gratitude took expression by sharing the good news about the child with anyone desirous of salvation. She, like Simeon, was given a special grace as she approached death.

Refrain: *"We sing your praises, holy Mother of God: you gave birth to our Savior, Jesus Christ; watch over all who honor you."*

GRATEFULNESS

Thou that hast giv'n so much to me,
Give one thing more, a grateful heart.
See how thy beggar works on thee
      By art.

He makes thy gifts occasion more,
And says, If he in this be crossed,
All thou hast giv'n him heretofore
      Is lost.

But thou didst reckon, when at first
Thy word our hearts and hands did crave,
What it would come to at the worst
      To save.

Perpetual knockings at thy door,
Tears sullying thy transparent rooms,
Gift upon gift, much would have more,
      And comes.

This notwithstanding, thou wentst on,
And didst allow us all our noise:
Nay thou hast made a sigh and groan
      Thy joys.

Not that thou hast not still above
Much better tunes, than groans can make;
But that these country-airs thy love
        Did take.

Wherefore I cry, and cry again;
And in no quiet canst thou be,
Till I a thankful heart obtain
        Of thee:

Not thankful, when it pleaseth me;
As if thy blessings had spare days:
But such a heart, whose pulse may be
        Thy praise.

George Herbert

During the Octave of Christmas it is well to review the gifts we received at Christmas. But there is one gift in particular which is of supreme importance—the gift of a grateful heart. This gift is not wrapped, has no weight, has never been seen. But when it is present everyone can feel it, for it shines with radiance and joy.

Gratitude lived turns into praise. A grateful heart is a catalyst transforming our souls into worlds of praise. In this maturing process as we no longer focus on gifts but rejoice in the presence of the Giver, our souls burst into glory and praise. Anna was grateful; more, Anna in her fasting and prayer, glorified her God.

1. What does having a grateful heart mean to me?

2. When gifts are removed, can I still praise the Giver?

3. How did I identify with the "beggar" in the poem?

Praying with the Church
All powerful God,
may the human birth of your Son
free us from our former slavery to sin
and bring us new life.
We ask this through our Lord Jesus Christ, your Son,
who lives and reigns with you and the Holy Spirit,
one God, for ever and ever.

SEVENTH DAY in the OCTAVE of CHRISTMAS
December 31
John 1:1–18

The first page of a book opens a new world. The reader plunges in and life is often never the same. And God's book! Reading the Bible discloses God revealing. So we open John's Gospel and within moments we are immersed in mystery: creation, incarnation, trinity, love. If we heed these words and allow them to toughen our soul, all will be made new. A light will shine in our darkness and we will see the glory of God.

Refrain: *"Blessed is the womb which bore you, O Christ, and the breast that nursed you, Lord and Savior of the world, alleluia."*

THE H. SCRIPTURES II

Oh that I knew how all thy lights combine,
  And the configurations of their glory!
    Seeing not only how each verse doth shine,
But all the constellations of the story.
This verse marks that, and both do make a motion
    Unto a third, that ten leaves off doth lie:
      Then as dispersed herbs do watch a potion,
These three make up our Christian's destiny:
Such are thy secrets, which my life makes good,
    And comments on thee: for in ev'ry thing
      Thy words do find me out, and parallels bring,
And in another make me understood.
      Stars are poor books, and oftentimes do miss:
        This book of stars lights to eternal bliss.

George Herbert

When God's work finds us out we are given secrets that will guide us to our Christian destiny. When God's Word finds us out, we are saved. The scriptures tell the constellations of the story and these stories illumine our path. The plot is always the same: God's enduring love.

The stars were once good books, especially *the* star Polaris. But our physical geography helps us just to get home. Scripture, the book of divine stars, points us to eternal bliss. This is a holy book that ends in configurations of glory.

1. What are my five favorite scriptural passages?

2. What secrets have the scriptures revealed to me during this Christmas season?

3. What does John's Prologue tell me about God? About myself?

Praying with the Church
Father,
source of light in every age,
the virgin conceived and bore your Son
who is called Wonderful God, Prince of Peace.
May her prayer, the gift of a mother's love,
be your people's joy through all ages.
May her response, born of a humble heart,
draw your Spirit to rest on your people
Grant this through Christ our Lord.

EIGHTH DAY in the OCTAVE of CHRISTMAS
January 1: Mary, The Mother of God
or: SUNDAY in the OCTAVE of CHRISTMAS
Holy Family
Matthew 2:13–15,19–23 (A); Luke 2:22–40 (B); Luke 2:41–52 (C)

A week ago we celebrated the birth of the Lord; today we honor the Holy Family, this trinity of persons who wandered down to Egypt in great hardship, who came to the temple in prayer and consecration, who sought the young Jesus and found him instructing the teachers. Joys and sorrows, tears and fears, life and death shared on common journey, around a common table. And with the family the experience of a God whose creative, redeeming, and sanctifying power could be duly felt.

Refrain: "*Son, why have you done this to us? Think what anguish your father and I have endured looking for you. But why did you look for me? Did you not know that I had to be in my Father's house?*"

TRINITY SUNDAY

Lord, who hast form'd me out of mud,
    And hast redeem'd me through thy blood,
    And sanctifi'd me to do good;

Purge all my sins done heretofore:
    For I confess my heavy score,
    And I will strive to sin no more.

Enrich my heart, mouth, hands in me,
    With faith, with hope, with charity;
    That I may run, rise, rest with thee.

George Herbert

Two great mysteries ground Christianity: the Incarnation and the Trinity. Jesus is born of Mary. Together with Joseph they shared the muddiness of human existence, felt the sanctifying power of the Spirit, prepared for the day when Jesus' self-sacrifice would redeem the world. The Holy Family saw sin in Herod's massacre. They saw grace in people of faith, hope, and charity.

    This Holy Family knew from experience the cycle of life and death. And always it was back to the temple, back into the mystery of a providential and loving God. God came to them in Simeon and Anna, in the religious festivals, in daily grace. This family ran, rose and rested in the very life of God.

    1. What role does faith play in my family? In my relationships?

2. How do I experience the mystery of the Trinity?

3. What was the greatest grace I received from my parents?

Praying with the Church
Father in heaven, creator of all,
you ordered the earth to bring forth life
and crowned its goodness by creating the family of man.
In history's moment when all was ready,
you sent your Son to dwell in time,
obedient to the laws of life in our world.
Teach us the sanctity of human love,
show us the value of family life,
and help us to live in peace with all people
that we may share in your life for ever.
We ask this through Christ our Lord.

WEEKDAY of CHRISTMASTIDE
January 2
John 1:19–28

To know who you are and what your purpose in life is—
what a double grace! John the Baptist understood himself to be simply a voice in the desert and his mission to be one of preparation. No claim to messiahship, no assuming Elijah's personality, no prophetic mantle, John's baptism with water pointed to a greater baptism by Jesus. We are in deep mysteries here, far beyond limited human comprehension.

Refrain: "*O radiant child! You brought healing to human life as you came forth from the womb of Mary, your mother, like the bridegroom from his marriage chamber.*"

BEYOND ME

"*Most things are beyond me. I ain't found anything yet that I thoroughly understood.*"
(*Dr. Block in Flannery O'Connor's "The Enduring Chill"*)

It's beyond me:
The Lemming's long march to the sea;
how satellites stay in perfect orbit,
blindly obedient to technology; the
fidelity of animals, the infidelity of man;
why the funny bone laughs at incongruity.

Way beyond me the mysteries of the heavens,
galaxies without numbers, angels famous who
dance on pin heads, the majesty of God,
a God-made-man.

Yet one thing I thoroughly understand—
that most things are beyond me.
And to understand one's ignorance
is to be wise indeed.

Robert F. Morneau

When things are beyond us—the Incarnation, the Trinity, the glorious feast of Epiphany—we turn to faith. John the Baptist was a man of faith. Far beyond him were the politics of his day. Yet he responded to what God asked of him in the here and now—true wisdom indeed.

John thoroughly understood one thing: he was not the Messiah. He knew himself as creature and servant, sent to prepare minds and hearts for the coming of the Redeemer. There is a blessed humility which empowers us to say we don't know or fully understand. And, of course, beyond us is the mystery of God ever driving us into the divine tent.

1. What three things do I think I really understand?

2. How are we to imitate the mission of John the Baptist?

3. Today would be a good day to renew baptismal promises.

Praying with the Church

Lord,
keep us true in the faith,
proclaiming that Christ your Son,
who is one with you in eternal glory,
became man and was born of a virgin mother.
Free us from all evil
and lead us to the joy of eternal life.
We ask this through our Lord Jesus Christ, your Son,
who lives and reigns with you and the Holy Spirit,
one God, for ever and ever.

WEEKDAY of CHRISTMASTIDE
January 3
John 1:29–34

Recognizing God is no easy task. Even John the Baptist, his whole life given to preparing the way of the Lord, admits that the divine disguise threw him off. But the day came and John exclaimed: "Look there! The Lamb of God who takes away the sin of the world!" This testimony of God's chosen one came through the grace of the Holy Spirit. Indeed,we can dance with delight and permit our hearts to rejoice. God is not dead.

Refrain: "Let us dance with delight in the Lord and let our hearts be filled with rejoicing, for eternal salvation has appeared on the earth, alleluia."

NIETZSCHE'S GOD

So, God is dead.
I heard the whimper of the maddening crowd,
its falsetto laughter, its terror of transience.
When did the Deity die?
In the darkness of the Enlightenment?
In the illness of the Renaissance?
In the madness of Rationalism?
I could find no divine corpse
though the "*Dies irae*" reached my ears.
I could smell no incense nor hear a tolling bell,
though the church was filled with unbelieving mourners.
God is dead?
Nietzsche's haunting words still live.

Robert F. Morneau

John's "look there" is countered by Nietzsche: "look nowhere!" Modern philosophers have declared God is dead as they plunge into the darkness of agnosticism. Once again reason and faith have been torn asunder. Reality is too large for our finite brains, and so what cannot be controlled is denied existence.

Like John, we need the Spirit to help us see God and follow in the footsteps of Christ. But it will take admission of sin as a prerequisite for the seeing. When sin is denied, the next chapter will surely be the death of God.

1. Where do I "see" God? Where do I look?

2. In what ways does our culture live as though God were dead?

3. How do I keep God "alive" in my life?

Praying with the Church
　　God our Father,
　　when your Son was born of the Virgin Mary
　　he became like us in all things but sin.
　　May we who have been reborn in him
　　be free from our sinful ways.
　　We ask this through our Lord Jesus Christ, your Son,
　　who lives and reigns with you and the Holy Spirit,
　　one God, for ever and ever.

WEEKDAY of CHRISTMASTIDE
January 4
John 1:35–42

A good Gospel question: "What are you looking for?" A good question from any point of view. To name one's desires is to be in touch with deep things. And to be in touch with the soul gives quality, maybe even holiness, to our days. Jesus says to Andrew and us: "Come and see." If we see deeply into the life of Jesus, we will come to know what we are looking for. Perhaps we are looking for love, looking to be lovers—divine maniacs.

Refrain: "I have come forth from God into the world; I have not come of myself, but the Father sent me."

MANIACS
"Lovers, inventors and artists are maniacs." (Michael Heim)

Am I one of them, or,
God forbid, all three?
Are they all mad?
These rebels against time and space.
But—what's the alternative?
A sameness numbing everyone to slow death.
A tameness caging the eagle from the sky.
If life demands death
—or so the grain of wheat was told—
does holy sanity demand divine madness?
Lovers now lost in the beloved,
inventors one with a new creation,
artists consumed by stones or words or colors.
And the divine comedy goes on.

Robert F. Morneau

Lovers by definition lose themselves in each other; inventors play at being God; and artists, a hopeless lot, are caught up in the abstractions of form and color and line. Add to the list apostles and disciples and we are in a mad, mad world.

Yet all these "professionals" are called to submission. And to be under the mission of Jesus is the happiest of madnesses. It will mean death, don't doubt it. It will also mean the risen life. Not to be a maniac is to miss the point of life. What we are all looking for is a Master of love and forgiveness. The sane don't even see the need to seek.

1. Do I consider myself a maniac? Why/why not?

2. Are any of my friends lovers, inventors, or artists?

3. Why are saints "other world" people?

Praying with the Church
All-powerful Father,
you sent your Son Jesus Christ
to bring the new light of salvation to the world.
May he enlighten us with his radiance,
who lives and reigns with you and the Holy Spirit,
one God, for ever and ever.

WEEKDAY of CHRISTMASTIDE
January 5
John 1:43–51

Four great knights of faith: Andrew, Peter, Philip, Nathaniel. And through the years great women of faith: Monica of Hippo, Catherine of Siena, Teresa of Avila, Julian of Norwich. All of them responded to the "Come, see for yourself." They came, they saw, and *their hearts were* conquered. They met Jesus, the epiphany of God's love and mercy, and they believed.

Refrain: "We have found Jesus of Nazareth, the son of Joseph. He is the one of whom Moses and the prophets wrote."

KIERKEGAARD'S KNIGHT OF FAITH

Envy struck my faint heart
in learning of this Knight of Faith,
I, a mere Serf of Night.
The Knight's armor truly shining:
trust in invisible realms of light and love,
courage to face pettiness, adventure with the same breath,
generous to damsels and rogues in distress,
acceptance, a centered "yes," to all that is.
By contrast to this daylight noble,
my paltryness knows no bounds,
my fears dreading high adventure that demands sacrifice,
my center being at home, not in transcendent realms above.

How does one in the night get knighted?
Is it a sudden grace, like lightning,
or gradual, stealing in like the dawn?

Robert F. Morneau

Jesus seeks us out no matter where we are: under a fig tree, atop a sycamore, sitting at the end of a bar, mowing hay in the meadow. And the message is always the same: "Follow me" into realms of light and love, to those in pain and distress, in the valley of tears and up the mountains of transcendence and transfiguration.

But following means leaving. Knights of yore ventured forth in courage. We pilgrims too must face the night and seek to hear and respond to the voice of the Lord. Allegiance is everything. We follow the banner of the kingdom committed to truth and love, freedom and justice. And with the dawn, the knights and ladies of faith rejoice.

1. How does my faith find expression?

2. Where has the Lord found and spoken to me on the faith journey?

3. What are the signs indicating that we are following Jesus?

Praying with the Church
Father,
you make known the salvation of mankind
at the birth of your Son.
Make us strong in faith
and bring us to the glory you promise.
We ask this through our Lord Jesus Christ, your Son,
who lives and reigns with you and the Holy Spirit,
one God, for ever and ever.

WEEKDAY of CHRISTMASTIDE
January 6
Mark 1:7–11

There are certain places where time and eternity intersect. When Jesus came to the Jordan River and heard, "You are my beloved Son. On you my favor rests," he stood at one of those intersections. And there were others: the Upper Room, Gethsemane, Calvary. At these places and in those moments, identity was felt and realized. These are the chapters in our history of epiphanies.

Refrain: "He came through blood and water, Jesus Christ our Lord."

ALDERSGATE STREET
(8:45 p.m., 24 May 1738)

Time and place: intersections of grace.
God's warming of hearts,
  imbuing assurance where doubt reigned before,
instilling trust in a trembling soul.
Sin snatched away,
  death defanged by this eternal moment.
Faith the gift that filled the night,
and perfect love one's life's work.
Would that I too could journal:
"I felt my heart strangely warmed"—
but then where is Aldersgate Street?

Robert F. Morneau

It was John Wesley who, on May 24, 1738, encountered God at Aldersgate Street. Like St. Paul, this was a touchstone experience changing their personal history in a dramatic way. God continues to work in the present as much as in the past. At the Jordan River, on the road to Damascus, at Aldersgate Street, grace was operative. It is also operative on January 6 and in the silence of our heart.

The challenge is one of attentiveness. We are in need of sensitive spiritual antennae that pick up the signs of transcendence. Surrounded by epiphanies, we need but look and listen intently to experience the continuing advent of our God. And then, of course, we must respond appropriately.

1. Have I had any Jordan River experiences or Aldersgate Street experiences?

2. How do I develop sensitive spiritual antennae?

3. Are intersections of grace different from intrusions of grace?

Praying with the Lord
Lord,
fill our hearts with your light.
May we always acknowledge Christ as our Savior
and be more faithful to his gospel,
for he lives and reigns with you and the Holy Spirit,
one God, for ever and ever.

WEEKDAY of CHRISTMASTIDE
January 7
John 2:1–12

There are certain words that echo down the centuries. For Christians, five words come from Mary's statement at Cana: "Do whatever he tells you." The waiters followed her injunction and we know the happy results. Down through the centuries all the great holy women and men did the same and brought about various facets of the kingdom. The choicest wine is that of obedience for it alone leads to life and liberty. And, let it be known, to happiness.

Refrain: "He is the one of whom it has been written: Christ is born in Israel; his kingdom will last for ever."

PRESENCE
"there is a third silent party to all our bargains." (Emerson)

> It seemed but two,
> a seller and a buyer.
> Who invited justice?
>
> The phone rang,
> just a caller and a listener.
> How did truth get on the party line?
>
> The groom kissed the bride,
> that's all the photo showed.
> How did God get filmed?

Robert F. Morneau

At Cana in Galilee there were surely more than two. Indeed, a whole crowd gathered here, including Jesus and his celebrating followers. But as the water became wine, it became obvious that the miracle spoke of the mystery of God, a God who is part of all our transactions and bargains.

Even when we are alone a silent party pursues us, whispering instructions that lead to justice, truth, and love. Were we able to have a camera sensitive enough to capture all reality, we would see, perhaps even hear, the eternal presence and providence of our loving God. The Boy Scouts have got it right: "Be prepared." And Mary certainly had it right: "Do whatever he tells you."

1. Who is the third party in my daily life?

2. On this January 7th, what is the Lord telling me to do?

3. What are the choice wines in my life? Is obedience one of them?

Praying with the Church
   All powerful and ever-living God,
   you give us a new vision of your glory
   in the coming of Christ your Son.
   He was born of the Virgin Mary
   and came to share our life.
   May we come to share his eternal life
   in the glory of your kingdom,
   where he lives and reigns with you and the Holy Spirit,
   one God, for ever and ever.

FEAST OF
THE EPIPHANY

Matthew 2:1–12

T. S. Eliot, in his writing about the Magi's coming to
Bethlehem, raised the question as to whether or not
they experienced birth or death. And the question goes
deeper: is there a difference between these two human
experiences? Gifts of gold, frankincense, and myrrh were
given to the infant. The Magi had to make a response to
their experience of new life, a new manifestation of God's
love for humankind. Already at the birth of Jesus we are
given intimations that God's love is extravagant and will
manifest itself in moments of new life and in death, sym-
bolized by the myrrh.

*Refrain: "Seeing the star, the wise men said: This must signify the
birth of some great king. Let us search for him and lay our treasures
at his feet: gold, frankincense and myrrh."*

MARKINGS

On the Mississippi—mark twain!
If heading toward Oz—the yellow brick road!
When the British come—one if by land, two . . .

What are the markings for your soul?
Are the longitudes and latitudes true co-ordinates?
And when you do get lost—what then?

I look to Polaris and head due north!
I listen for the wind of the Spirit—Joy—and dance!
I lean into God's word and find a lamp unto my feet.

Robert F. Morneau

If there were an Epiphany, a manifestation, then there must be markings whereby we know something specific about the happenings. It seems that divine epiphanies are marked by song, whether sung by angels or shepherds or bus boys or migrant workers. Then there is the marking of hope, a star shining in the darkness of the night. Throw in a few gifts and you have a fairly good map to make your way into meaning.

The feast of Epiphany is about the mystery of love. Two elements always accompany love and are essential elements: light and life. In Jesus we are given the Light of the world and the very gift of Life itself, grace. What has been revealed is to be internalized and then shared. Each follower of Jesus is to become an epiphany.

The true co-ordinates of the soul lie in the longitude of joy and the latitude of peace. The Magi returned to their homeland hands emptied but souls filled. In giving their material gifts they created room for spiritual blessings. The markings of Epiphany are the peace and joy that come from encountering God-made-man.

1. How am I an epiphany for others?
2. What markings indicate to me the presence of love?
3. Are peace and joy more valuable than silver or gold?

Praying with the Church

    Father of light, unchanging God,
    today you reveal to men of faith
    the resplendent fact of the Word made flesh.
    Your light is strong,
    your love is near;
    draw us beyond the limits which this world imposes,
    to the life where your Spirit makes all life complete.
    We ask this through Christ our Lord.

ACKNOWLEDGMENTS

The author and the publisher wish to thank the following for permission to include previously published material:

For the English translation of the antiphons from *The Roman Missal* © 1973, International Committee on English in the Liturgy, Inc. (ICEL); the English translation of the prayers from *The Liturgy of the Hours* © 1974, ICEL. All rights reserved.

From *Selected Poetry of Jessica Powers*, edited by Regina Siegfried, ASC and Robert F. Morneau (Kansas City, Missouri: Sheed & Ward, 1989), 81. Reprinted with permission of the publisher.

From *Worship*, by Evelyn Underhill (New York: Crossroad, 1989), 113.

"Journey of the Magi," from *Collected Poems 1909–1962* by T. S. Eliot (New York: Harcourt Brace and Company, copyright © 1964, 1963 by T. S. Eliot), 99–100.

From *The Complete Poems of Emily Dickinson*, edited by Thomas H. Johnson (Boston: Little Brown and Company, 1960), Poems # 501 and 1129. Reprinted by permission of the publisher. From *Emily Dickinson Face to Face*, edited by Martha Dickinson Bianchi, Copyright 1932 by Martha Dickinson Bianchi, © renewed 1960 by Alfred Leete Hampson, Poem # 809. Reprinted by permission of Houghton Mifflin Co. All Rights reserved. Poems # 254, 324, 501, 764, 809, 919, and 1129 are reprinted by permission of the publishers and the Trustees of Amherst College from *The Poems of Emily Dickinson*, Thomas H. Johnson, ed., Cambridge, Mass.: The Belknap Press of Harvard University Press, Copyright © 1951, 1955, 1979, 1983 by the President and Fellows of Harvard College.

From *Times Alone, Selected Poems of Antonio Machado*, edited and translated by Robert Bly (Middletown, Connecticut: University Press of New England, 1983), 35, 43, 45, 57, 109, 133, 149. Reprinted with permission of the publisher and Robert Bly.

From *Selected Poems of Rainer Maria Rilke*, edited and translated by Robert Bly (New York: Harper & Row, 1981), 23, 31, 39, 41, 105–106. Copyright © 1981 by Robert Bly. Reprinted by permission of Harper Collins Publishers, Inc.

From *George Herbert, The Complete English Works*, edited and introduced by Ann Pasternak Slater (New York: Everyman's Library, Alfred A. Knopf, 1995), 5, 34, 56, 64–65, 108–109, 120–21.

"Faith," "Veni Creator," "Incantation," "An Hour," "On Angels," "My-ness," "Secretaries," "Gift," and "Thankfulness" from *The Collected Poems 1931–1987* by Czeslaw Milosz. Copyright © 1988 by Czeslaw Milosz Royalties, Inc. Reprinted by permission of The Ecco Press.